GETTING TO KNOW
THE WORLD'S
GREATEST COMPOSERS

JOHN   PHILIP
SOUSA

WRITTEN AND ILLUSTRATED BY MIKE VENEZIA

CHILDREN'S PRESS®
A DIVISION OF GROLIER PUBLISHING
NEW YORK   LONDON   HONG KONG   SYDNEY
DANBURY, CONNECTICUT

For my editor, Russell Primm.
Thanks for all your support and dinners in Chinatown.

Picture Acknowledgements
Photographs ©:Brown Brothers: 3, 17; Stock Montage, Inc.: 11; The Barry Owen Furrer Collection of John Philip Sousa Memorabilia: 6, 7, 20, 22, 23, 25, 30; United States Marine Band: 12, 18; United States Marine Band: 10 (Matthew Brady); UPI/Corbis-Bettmann: 32.

Visit Children's Press on the Internet at:
http://publishing.grolier.com

Library of Congress Cataloging-in-Publication Data

Venezia, Mike.
    John Philip Sousa / written and illustrated by Mike Venezia.
       p. cm. -- (Getting to know the world's greatest composers)
    Summary: A simple biography of the famous band leader and composer
      who was known as the March King.
    ISBN 0-516-20761-X (lib. bdg.)   0-516-26401-X (pbk.)
    1. Sousa. John Philip. 1854-1932--Juvenile literature.
    2. Composers--United States--Biography--Juvenile literature.
    [1. Sousa. John Philip. 1854-1932. 2. Composers. 3. Musicians.]
    I. Title. II. Series: Venezia, Mike. Getting to know the world's
      greatest composers.
ML3930.S7V46 1998
784.8'3'092--dc21
  [B]   98-23298
                                                CIP
                                         MN AC

American composer John Philip Sousa was known as the March King.

John Philip Sousa was born in Washington, D.C., the capital of the United States of America, in 1854. He always loved his country and showed his love by writing some of the most original and patriotic music ever.

John Philip Sousa is best known for his
thrilling marches. The unusual titles he gave
them may be unfamiliar to some people today.
But almost everyone has heard *El Capitan,
The Washington Post, High School Cadets,
Manhattan Beach, King Cotton,* and *Semper
Fidelis* at one time or another. These marches
are always being played in movies, tv shows,
parades, and by school bands.

John Philip Sousa said that when he
wanted to write a march, he would sometimes
try to imagine scenes of battles with rifles
firing and cannons exploding. He would
hear the clanking of swords and the sound
of soldiers marching to the drum beat.
All of a sudden, a tune would come to him.
He was always amazed how this happened.

The cover of some sheet music from Sousa's operetta *El Capitan*

Sousa also composed music for operettas. An operetta is a short, usually comic play in which the actors sing and dance their parts as the orchestra plays along. John Philip Sousa was proud of the music he wrote for these plays. He liked some of it better than some of the marches he composed. John couldn't understand why his operetta music

Sheet-music covers for three of Sousa's many marches

never became as popular as his marches. It was always a disappointment to him.

efore John Philip Sousa was born, the United States didn't really have music it could call its own. The United States was a fairly new country, and American composers had not yet become well known.

In big cities, people went to concerts and listened to the work of European composers, like Bach, Beethoven, and Mozart. Tickets to these concerts were expensive, and people had to dress in fancy clothes to get in. Everyone was pretty snobby about the whole thing. In the rest of the country, people had to listen to bands and

musical entertainers who weren't very good
a lot of the time. Everybody wanted to hear
music so much though, that they were happy
to accept anything that came along.

While John Philip Sousa was growing
up, he was lucky to be able to listen to
the many military bands that played in
Washington, D.C. At that time, the Civil War
was going on. Washington, D.C., was almost
like an armed camp and was under attack at
times by Confederate soldiers. Army bands
were all over the place. They were needed to

The United States Marine Band in the 1860s, during the Civil War

A Civil War battle

announce daily activities or send commands
and signals. They were also an important way
of keeping soldiers happy during long, boring
marches. Sometimes bands would play old,
familiar songs that reminded soldiers of
happier times. These military bands made
a deep impression on John Philip Sousa.

John Philip Sousa's
parents

John Philip Sousa grew up in a musical family. His father played the trombone in the United States Marine Band. Mr. Sousa encouraged his son to take violin lessons at an early age. He taught him to play the trombone and other band instruments as well.

Soon John's parents and teachers knew John had a special musical talent. When he was only eleven years old, John put together a dance band that played in the Washington, D.C., area. He was the leader of seven grown men, and the band became pretty popular.

When John Philip Sousa was thirteen years old, the circus came to his town. One night, the owner of the circus heard John's dance band play. He really liked what he heard and asked John if he would like to join the circus and become their band leader.

John Philip Sousa thought traveling around the world with the circus would be a great idea! He decided to join up and run away from home. Fortunately, Mr. Sousa found out about the plan. The next morning, he marched his son down to the marine barracks and signed him up in the Marine Corps band. At the age of thirteen,

John Philip Sousa was a United States
Marine. He was also in a place where his
father could keep an eye on him.

At that time, the U.S. Marines were very different from the way they are today. Things weren't so strict. In fact, John and other band members could leave at the end of the day and play their instruments at dances or city concerts to make extra money.

John enjoyed his stay in the Marine Band and learned a lot. After seven years, though, he decided to leave. John felt there were musical opportunities outside the Marine Band where he could learn more and develop his talents.

John Philip Sousa as a young man

Jane Bellis Sousa,
John Philip Sousa's wife

John Philip Sousa began traveling to different cities where he played his violin and composed music. In one city, he met and fell in love with a singer from a theater group. Her name was Jane Bellis. John and Jane got married and soon after their wedding, an important thing happened. John Philip Sousa was asked to come back to the U.S. Marine Band. This time, though, it was not as a musician, but as their leader! John was glad to accept the job.

When John got back to Washington, D.C., however, he was disappointed to find the band in pretty bad shape. Many of the band members really didn't want to be there anymore. Their uniforms were worn out and the music they played seemed old and boring to John.

The front cover of a concert program for the first national concert tour by the U.S. Marine Band

John got to work right away. He decided to try to make this band the best military band in the world. He started by getting new and better musicians to join up, and he made them practice for long hours. He got rid of a lot of the dull music the band was used to playing, and replaced it with more modern music by European and American composers. John added his own marches, too.

One of John's favorite assignments was to play for the president of the United States whenever he needed music for a party or special government affair.

John Philip Sousa got to meet five different presidents during the time he was the leader of the Marine Band. During this time he also wrote some of his best marches, including *Semper Fidelis* and *The Washington Post.* He even became known as the March King.

The U.S. Marine Band became more popular than ever before. Sometimes thousands of people would gather for its concerts. One day after

a concert, a businessman named David Blakely talked to John Philip Sousa about starting up his own band. John liked the idea. He thought that if he had his own band, he could travel more and play his great music for people all over the United States, or even all over the world. He could choose all his favorite pieces to play and make a lot more money, too. In 1892, he left the marines to start his very own band.

The U.S. Marine Band as led by John Philip Sousa (center)

After twelve years of leading the U.S. Marine Band, John Philip Sousa knew exactly how to put a successful band together. He started by hiring the best musicians he could find. He spent weeks rehearsing and training them. He made sure they had the coolest-looking uniforms, too. John knew his band would have to look great as well as sound great.

David Blakely became John's partner and manager. He made sure the band was set up to play in different cities and took care of advertising.

When John was done putting the band together, it turned out to be a combination symphony orchestra and concert band. Sousa's band hardly ever marched, but they could play any type of music, from simple American folk songs to big, famous symphonies.

John Philip Sousa formed his own concert band in 1892.

From the very beginning, John Philip Sousa's band was a big hit! He always made sure he played music that everyone could enjoy. There were never any snobby feelings when the Sousa Band played.

John and his band traveled to as many cities and towns as possible. It was almost like a big holiday when they came to town. Schools and businesses closed, and everyone from miles around would go to the concert. Sometimes the audience loved the music so much that they demanded the band play their favorite piece over and over again. John Philip Sousa never minded doing this, especially if they wanted to hear one of his marches.

John Philip Sousa's marches were and still are popular all over the world. The idea for his most famous march, *The Stars and Stripes Forever,* came to him while he was traveling on an ocean liner in 1896. Later, John remembered how clearly he had heard an imaginary band play *The Stars and Stripes Forever* in his head as the

rough sea bounced his ship back and forth.
John believed this piece was inspired by God.
As soon as he got home, he wrote the notes
down exactly as he heard them. The powerful
rhythms of this patriotic march have made
people so proud of being American that they
often stand while this song is being played.

The Stars and Stripes Forever did just what John Philip Sousa thought a good march should do, which was make goose bumps chase each other up and down your back when you listen to it. Even when his band played *The Stars and Stripes Forever* in other countries, it gave people the same kind of proud feeling as it did in the United States.

For many years, John Philip Sousa and
his band were among the most famous
entertainers in the world. Wherever John
went, kings, queens, presidents, and mayors
of towns honored him. John was given so
many medals, he could never wear them
all at the same time.

John Philip Sousa leading a naval marching band during World War I

John Philip Sousa lived to be seventy-seven years old. During a time when radio and television were not yet around, he made it possible for thousands of people all over to hear good music. He helped show how important American composers were by playing their compositions in different countries around the world. He always had fun playing music, but treated each musical piece as if it were the most important one ever, whether it was a simple street tune or great symphony.